For Walter and Molly

~

FOREWORD

One of my favourite artists is Jan Vermeer. There was a small print of his painting *The Maid With The Milk Jug* on the wall in a dark passage in my grandmother's house. It was part of the furniture so I took it for granted, but I never forgot it. I have included it here in this book of paintings.

I began to play 'I Spy' with paintings with my own children when they were very young. As we looked into each picture we found much that was familiar and a great deal that was unfamiliar. Often children pointed out things which I had never noticed – an apple that had fallen to the floor, a funny-shaped shoe, the wind in the grass, a pattern on the carpet. They helped me to remember how to look and see and judge for myself.

Most art books live on the top shelf, out of reach, but this one is for the picture book shelf. It contains a handful of paintings for you to explore. I hope you will like them and have fun getting to know them.

Lucy Micklethwait 1991

Cover picture: René Magritte, *The Great War* (1964)
Private Collection

Title page picture: Georges Seurat, *Sunday Afternoon on the Island of La Grande Jatte* (1884-86)

I SPY

An Alphabet In Art

Devised & selected by Lucy Micklethwait

Collins

An Imprint of HarperCollinsPublishers

I spy
with my little eye
something beginning with

Aa

René Magritte, *Son of Man*

I spy
with my little eye
something beginning with

Henri Rousseau, *Football Players*

I spy
with my little eye
something beginning with

Cc

William Hogarth, *The Graham Children*

I spy
with my little eye
something beginning with

Dd

I spy
with my little eye
something beginning with

Ee

Indian, *Workmen Building the Palace of Fatehpur Sikri*

I spy
with my little eye
something beginning with

Ff

Pablo Picasso, *Sitting Woman with a Fish Hat*

I spy
with my little eye
something beginning with

Gg

Follower of Jan van Kessel, *Still Life with Fruit and Flowers*

I spy
with my little eye
something beginning with

Hh

I spy
with my little eye
something beginning with

Ii

I spy
with my little eye
something beginning with

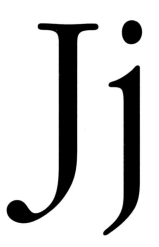

Jan Vermeer, *The Maid with the Milk Jug*

I spy
with my little eye
something beginning with

Kk

Jan Steen, *The World Upside Down*

I spy
with my little eye
something beginning with

Ll

John Singer Sargent, *Carnation, Lily, Lily, Rose*

I spy
with my little eye
something beginning with

Mm

EL S.^{D.n} MANVEL OSORIO MANRRIQ^E D ZVÑIGA S.^D D GIN^E NA...

I spy
with my little eye
something beginning with

Nn

Jan van Huijsum, *Flowers in a Vase*

I spy
with my little eye
something beginning with

Oo

Henri Matisse, *Interior with Etruscan Vase*

I spy
with my little eye
something beginning with

Pp

Carlo Crivelli, *The Annunciation with St. Emidius*

I spy
with my little eye
something beginning with

Thomas Warrender, *Still Life*

I spy
with my little eye
something beginning with

Rr

I spy
with my little eye
something beginning with

Ss

Joan Miró, *Woman and Bird in the Moonlight*

I spy
with my little eye
something beginning with

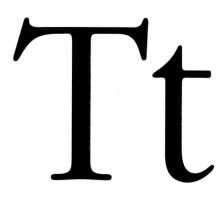

Jacob Savery II, *The Animals Entering Noah's Ark*

I spy
with my little eye
something beginning with

Uu

Pierre Auguste Renoir, *Umbrellas*

I spy
with my little eye
something beginning with

Vv

Marc Chagall, *The Bride and Groom of the Eiffel Tower*

I spy
with my little eye
something beginning with

Ww

David Hockney, *A Bigger Splash*

I spy
with my little eye
something ending with

Xx

The Limbourg Brothers, *March: Peasants at work on a feudal estate*

I spy
with my little eye
something beginning with

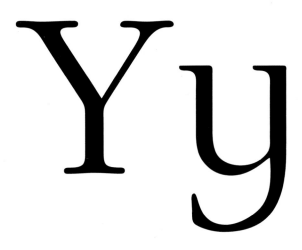

Yy

Georges Seurat, *Sunday Afternoon on the Island of La Grande Jatte*

I spy
with my little eye
something beginning with

Zz

Wybrand de Geest, *Portrait of a Boy with a Golf Club*

— I Spied With My Little Eye —

A apple
René Magritte (1898-1967), *Son of Man* (1964)
Private Collection

B ball
Henri Rousseau (1844-1910), *Football Players* (1908)
The Solomon R Guggenheim Museum, New York

C cat
William Hogarth (1697-1764), *The Graham Children* (1742)
The National Gallery, London

D dog
Jan van Eyck (working 1422, died 1441), *The Arnolfini Marriage* (1434)
The National Gallery, London

E elephants
Indian, *Workmen Building the Palace of Fatehpur Sikri* from *The Akbarnama*
(about 1590)
The Victoria and Albert Museum, London

F fish
Pablo Picasso (1881-1973), *Sitting Woman with a Fish Hat* (1942)
Stedelijk Museum, Amsterdam

G guinea pigs
Follower of Jan van Kessel (1626-1679), *Still Life with Fruit and Flowers on a Table*
The Harold Samuel Collection, Corporation of London

H heart
Jean-Baptiste-Siméon Chardin (1699-1779), *The House of Cards* (about 1735)
National Gallery of Art, Washington; Andrew W Mellon Collection

I inkwell
Sandro Botticelli (1445-1510), *Madonna of the Magnificat* (about 1482-1485)
The Uffizi Gallery, Florence

J jug

Jan Vermeer (1632-1675), *The Maid with the Milk Jug* (about 1660)

Rijksmuseum, Amsterdam

K key

Jan Steen (1626-1679), *The World Upside Down* (about 1663)

Kunsthistorisches Museum, Vienna

L lanterns

John Singer Sargent (1856-1925), *Carnation, Lily, Lily, Rose* (1885-1886)

The Tate Gallery, London

M magpie

Francisco Goya (1746-1828), *Don Manuel Osorio Manrique de Zuñiga* (born 1784)

The Metropolitan Museum of Art, New York; Jules Bache Collection

N nest

Jan van Huijsum (1682-1749), *Flowers in a vase* (1726)

The Wallace Collection, London

O oranges

Henri Matisse (1869-1954), *Interior with Etruscan Vase* (1940)

The Cleveland Museum Of Art, Gift of the Hanna Fund

P peacock

Carlo Crivelli (working 1457-1493), *The Annunciation with St. Emidius* (1486)

The National Gallery, London

Q quills

Thomas Warrender (working 1673-1713), *Still Life* (about 1708)

The National Gallery of Scotland, Edinburgh

R roses

Marcus Gheeraerts the Younger (working 1561, died 1635), *Queen Elizabeth I* (about 1592)

National Portrait Gallery, London

S stars

Joan Miró, (1893-1983) *Woman and Bird in the Moonlight* (1949)
The Tate Gallery, London

T turkey

Jacob Savery II (1593, died after 1627), *The Animals Entering Noah's Ark*
Private Collection

U umbrellas

Pierre Auguste Renoir (1841-1919), *Umbrellas* (about 1884)
The National Gallery, London

V violin

Marc Chagall (1887-1985), *The Bride and Groom of the Eiffel Tower*
(about 1939)
Musée National d'Art Moderne, Centre Georges Pompidou, Paris

W water

David Hockney (born 1937), *A Bigger Splash* (1967)
The Tate Gallery, London

X ox

The Limbourg Brothers (working 1411-1416), *March* from *Les Très Riches*
Heures du Duc de Berry (about 1415)
Musée Condé, Chantilly

Y yacht

Georges Seurat (1859-1891), *Sunday Afternoon on the Island of La Grande*
Jatte (1884-1886)
The Helen Bartlett Memorial Collection, Art Institute of Chicago

Z zigzag

Wybrand de Geest (1592-about 1660) *Portrait of a Boy with a Golf Club*
(1631)
Rijksmuseum, Amsterdam

I would like to thank all the children, parents, teachers, librarians, curators and friends who have contributed in some way or another and invariably with enthusiasm to this I Spy Alphabet.

ACKNOWLEDGEMENTS

Pictures are reproduced by courtesy of the galleries and museums listed at the back of this book and of the following:
The Bridgeman Art Library (E, G, I, K, T),
Photographie Giraudon (cover, A), Photographie Giraudon/Bridgeman Art Library (X)

A Bigger Splash © D Hockney 1967
Pablo Picasso *Sitting Woman with a Fish Hat*, René Magritte *The Great War* © D.A.C.S. 1992
René Magritte *Son of Man*, Joan Miró *Woman and Bird in the Moonlight*,
Marc Chagall *The Bride and Groom of the Eiffel Tower* © A.D.A.G.P., Paris and D.A.C.S., London 1992
Henri Matisse *Interior with Etruscan Vase* © Succession H Matisse/D.A.C.S. 1992

First published by HarperCollins in 1992
Compilation and text © Lucy Micklethwait 1992

ISBN 0 00 193715 4 (HB)
0 00 664184 9 (PB)

A CIP record for this title is available from the British Library

The author asserts the moral right to be identified as the author of the work.

Printed and bound in Great Britain